Authentic Peace

By Bonnie Bair

Life Improvements 2

Galesburg, Illinois

Names: Bair, Bonnie L. | Bair, Bonnie L. editor

Title: Authentic Peace | by Bonnie L. Bair

Description: 1st edition. | Galesburg, Illinois: Life
Improvements 2, 2021   Independently Published

Subject: Achieving Authentic Lasting Peace

Identifiers: LCCN 20219104102 print

ISBN 978-0-9994772-6-7

Foreword

In the garden of Eden, there was perfect peace, before the original sin of disobeying God and eating from the tree of the knowledge of good and evil. Knowing or practicing good and evil is not what we are supposed to do. We are not supposed to do evil that appears good. We are not supposed to have evil intent. Instead, we are to do good and shun evil.

Authentic Peace/Love

Acknowledges feeling of others/self

Acknowledges behavior/attitude of self

Serves one another cheerfully

Repents

Forgives

Prioritize God and others

Turn from evil and do good; seek peace and pursue it.
Psalm34:14 NIV

Counterfeit Peace/Love

Counterfeit/short-term peace is produced when **one agrees** with someone, just **to appear** in agreement (knowing in one's heart or mind, one plans to do something different than what they agreed to OR is resentful or hesitant in agreeing).

Also, it's **saying one thing and doing another.**

It produces **temporary peace** that **leads to strife and resentment** and future arguments or fighting.

It is **eating from the tree of knowledge of good and evil.** It is **practicing evil** while appearing good.

Creating Peace/Love – Long-term

- *Agrees with, and does, ONLY when a person is WILLING!*

- *Speaks/Acts in Truth*

- *Creates win/win/win situations/solutions with each other/God*

- *Adjusts thinking/behavior to line up with what God says.*

- *Increases*   Happiness   Satisfaction
            Trust   Contentment
        Connectedness   Freedom
        Honesty

Peacemakers who sow in peace reap a harvest of righteousness. James 3:18

10

Authentic Peace/Love

Speaks the truth in Love
Does what it says it will do!
Follows through!

Produces Peace/Love
Seeks to understand

Create Peace by:

Examples?

*Saying something nice, & truthful

*You are a good person because...

*I know you love me when ...

*Doing the right thing

I'm sorry I did not do as I promised. What can I do to make it up to you?

*Blessing Others – Do Not curse them!

*I realize I was stressed and may have sounded angry with you, when I was worried about ...

*You are important to me. I need you to understand my situation. Although I did not respond the way you would have liked, your happiness is important to me.

*Pray for others and self.

(Even w/a perceived threat or enemy)

Let your speech be a blessing,

*Cora looks out for her family

*Betty has a keen eye/notices details.

*As this is done, enemies will become your footstool.

Create Peace by:

How?

Imagine yourself in the other's shoes.

I can understand that. When I ..., I felt the same way.

I'm not sure what that would be like. Can you tell me more?

What might they need?

I can see you're in a tough spot, may I help With something or give a suggestion?

How might they feel?

That's a bummer! How frustrating!

Ask/Listen

You look sad. Would you like to talk?

Check it Out

You sound angry. Are you frustrated with me, or is it something else?

You look confused. Can I clarify something? How/what can I communicate more clearly?

(It will help you be more effective and successful.)

Blessed are the peacemakers, for they shall be called the children of God. Matthew 5:9 NIV

Create Peace by:

*Saying/Show Love/Acceptance

(for self, others, & God)

Acceptance, Words of praise,

Words of acknowledgment, effort,
thanksgiving, or acknowledgment of feelings.

Smile/Hug/Kiss/Handshake

Being Together

(Enjoying, Listening, Cooperating)

Doing something nice - serving

Giving a gift

Self-Discipline – doing what you

say you will do.

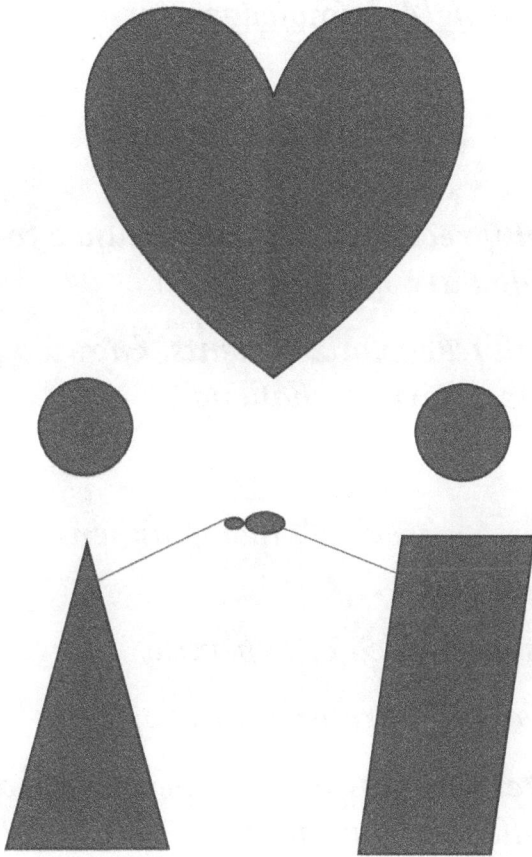

Appreciating/Acknowledgement

How?

*Verbally recognize the importance to you,
"You are my best friend."

* Verbally Recognize talents, knowledge, interests, efforts & challenges

"You do ____ well." "I like your sense of humor."

"This is your area of expertise."

"You worked hard on that project."

"You were successful in maneuvering around the challenges you faced."

Appreciation/Acknowledgement

How?

*Show appreciation

Make a special dinner

Share a gift, talent, or serve favorite cookies, sing a song, a foot massage, do the other's chore)

"Thank you!" (with a hug, ice cream, or card)

"Brenda said she liked your spaghetti. And so, did I!" (w/a smile)

"I love you!" (w/ a kiss, emoji, love note)

"You are so kind to me. You encourage me when I am sad. You charge my cell phone without me asking. You call the doctor when I am sick." (with a smile, hug, or gift)

Including Others

How?

*Show/Tell

"Did you get your car fixed?"

"Can I give you a ride somewhere?"

"Would you like to come over for dinner?"

"Would you like to join us at church or for a movie?"

"How can I help? What do you need?"

"Would you like a piece of cake?"

"I want to share my ____ with you."

"What are you up to?"

"Are you surviving the cold?" "Has your electricity stayed on?"

Cooperating w/others

How?

*Show/Tell

"You look, and sound stressed. Is there anything I can do to help?"

"You said you needed ... I am ordering it for you."

"You look cold. Would you like me to turn up the heat?"

"You said this was important. Do you have time to do this now? I am willing to do this while you do that, so we can get it done in time."

Honoring the other before yourself

*Ask about or check with the other person on what they are feeling and what they need, *before* you tell them what you feel and need.

(If you honor the other person first, the other person will be more open to listening to your feelings and needs.)

If the other person does not respond the way you want or need them to, after you tell them how you are feeling and what you are needing, you can handle the disappointment better because you acknowledged your feelings and needs, as well.

Chances are things went better for both of you because: 1) **You listened to and understood the other person** and 2) **You stated your needs**

Honoring the other person first helps keep the guesswork out of things. When you honor the other person first, there is less chance for misunderstandings, resentments, and misinterpretation of behavior to occur.

Love each other deeply. Honor others more than yourselves. *Romans 12:10 NIRV*

Loving Others while loving Ourselves

How to maintain ourselves (who we are), while serving others?

1. State how you understand the other person is feeling or what they are needing.
2. Tell the other person your feelings and needs (even if they don't ask)
3. Assume/Think the best of each other. (Perception affects behavior)
4. Tell yourself, and the other person, the truth. Acknowledge each other's position and efforts.
5. Think the best of each other.

We all want understanding love and respect, even when we don't agree or when our needs are conflicting.

Jesus said, "You shall love the Lord thy God will all thy heart, with all thy soul, and with all your mind, and thou shall love they neighbor as thyself."

Matt 22:37-39

How to say "No."

**First,** you have permission to say "No."

Say, "No," when necessary. (The more you practice, the easier it gets.)

> _If you can say it in a way you feel good about, it's best, so guilt does not set in. Say it with a tone of self-acceptance and without trying to make the other person feel bad for asking._

> _Acknowledging the other person's situation, or need, (as well as your own) is half the battle._

> _Stick with your answer!_

Let your yes be yes and your no, no. Whatever is more than these, is from the evil one. Matthew 5:37

Be true to yourself. Be kind to others. Speak the truth with a spirit/tone of love and acceptance.

Make every effort to live in peace with everyone and to be holy; without holiness, no one will see the Lord.
Hebrews 12:14 NIV

Summary

<u>Causes of Difficulty</u>

Perceiving Bad in self/others/God

Misunderstandings

Overgeneralizing/Exaggerating

Judging/Blaming

Excluding

Unwillingness/Resistence

Allowing evil to take over

Lying

<u>Causes of Peace</u>

Perceiving Good in self/others/God

Understanding

Accuracy in speech

Accepting   Including

Cooperation

Appreciation
Honesty

Spiritual Practices for Peaceful Relationships

Seeking God Daily

Thankfulness

Listening

Giving

Communication

Cooperation

Purity

Rest

Seeking God Daily - *helps us to be at peace.*

Blessed is the person who listens to me, watching daily at my doors, waiting at my doorway. For those who find me, find life. Those who fail to find me, harm themselves. Proverbs 8:34-36

A day that begins and ends in prayer, won't become unraveled. Psalms 92:1-2

God's word is a lamp to our feet and a light to our paths. Psalm 119:105

Thankfulness - *Helps us in our relationships with God and others. It causes peace.*

- *It helps us to focus on the good in our lives and each other.*

- *It helps us to appreciate.*

Let the peace of God rule in your hearts, to which you were called in one body, and become thankful. Colossians 3:1

Whatever is true, noble, right, pure, lovely, admirable – if anything is excellent or praiseworthy – think about such things. And the God of peace will be with you. Philippians 4:8 & 9

Listening –

   helps in our relationships to show we care.

  Taking turns, when listening, brings peace.

Men often like directness, with simplicity, in speech. It helps them to focus and follow.

Women like it when feelings are discussed and acknowledged.

  -Consider writing thoughts down to better organize and prepare for more direct and respectful communication.

  -Schedule talk times that are good for all individuals involved.

Listening

-*Seek to understand, before being understood.*

These affirmations create peace:

"*I listen to understand.*"

"*I acknowledge how the other person feels.*"

"*I think before I respond.*"

Everyone must be quick to hear, slow to speak, and slow to anger. James 1:19

Happy is the person who finds wisdom and gains understanding.

Prov 3:13

Giving – *Give, and it will be given to you.*
Luke 6:38

-*Mercy*

-*Forgiveness*

-*Understanding*

-*A physical Gift
(Item or Money)*

-*Time*

-*Service*

-*Smile
or Hug*

*When you give to another person,
consider what they value, want, and
need.*

He who refreshes others will also be refreshed.

Prov 11:25

Communication – *Seeking time with each other - enjoying and valuing each other brings peace.*

-Taking interest in each other

-Speaking the truth in a loving tone

-Cooperating when we can,

-Asking questions in a loving tone

-Acknowledging feelings, thoughts, and situations

-Signifying understanding

Examples of Communication

It appears you might be feeling confused. I'm feeling frustrated.

Would you be willing to listen to understand what I'm saying?

I need some time to calm down and get something to eat.

Do you mind if we talk after supper about this? That will help me to listen better.

I like when the house is kept clean. It helps me function better and feel peaceful.

Would you be willing to put things back where they belong?

Would you be willing to help me establish a home for certain items, so we can find them more easily?

I like when you help me make dinner. It keeps me company and I feel closer to you.

Cooperation – *Helps us to get things accomplished that we could not do independently. This creates peace.*

Negotiate

1. *Listen to and ask about the other person's needs, concerns, and ideas.*

2. *Consider the other person's needs, concerns, and ideas and state what you understand them to be.*

3. *State your own needs, concerns, and ideas.*

Let each of you look not only to his interests but also to the interests of others. Philippians 2:4

If this has caused fights in the past, try writing your thoughts down until you are better at verbally communicating and negotiating.

If one person's needs are deemed more important than the others regularly, destruction is sure to come. The peace will be short-lived and come at a cost.

Try your best to negotiate win/win situations and solutions, take turns, or agree to disagree.

Do two walk together, unless they have agreed to meet? Amos 3:3

Remember, agreeing with someone just to keep the peace, knowing in your heart or mind that you plan to do something different than what you agreed upon will cause problems.

Saying one thing and doing another is practicing both good and evil, it is counterfeit temporary peace.

Agreeing only when you can truly agree and keep your word, leads to more lasting reoccurring peace.

Keep judgment, guilt, and blame out of communication.

Instead, seek to understand, accept, and take responsibility for yourself and your communications.

How good and pleasant it is when brothers dwell in unity! Psalm 133:1

Purity/Innocence - *gives us a clear conscience and helps us to live at peace with others.*

- *Intention* – *good*
- *Thought* – *think the best of self/others*
- *Action* – *Be responsible*
- *Speech* – *truthful and kind*

Be as wise as serpents and as innocent as doves.
Matthew 10:16

Rest – stop working and do something enjoyable. It helps us to rejuvenate and recover. It creates peace.

- -An outing together or alone

- -A much-needed nap

- - A car or bike ride

- -Worship/Restoration

It gives us strength, enjoyment, a different perspective, time to reflect and plan.

It helps us be more pleasant to live with - which creates peace.

A sabbath-rest for the people of God; for anyone who enters God's rest also rests from their works, just as God rested. Hebrews 4:9-10

Summary of Authentic Peace

Connect with God Daily

Perceive the good in self/others/God

Agree to only that which you can truly agree with.

Be Accepting/Understanding

Be innocent

Speak kindly and truthfully

Include others

Appreciate

Cooperate

Listen

Communicate

Give

Rest

Peace I leave with you; my peace I give you. I do not give to you as the world gives. Do not let your hearts be troubled. Do not be afraid.

John 14:27

Make every effort to live in peace with everyone and to be holy; without holiness, no one will see the Lord. Hebrews 12:14 NIV

It is Satan that wants us to argue and be offended, not God.

We wrestle not against flesh and blood, but against evil forces. Ephesians 6:12

Resist the devil and he will flee from you. James 4:7

Greater is he that is in you, than he who is in the world. John 4:4

Do everything without complaining or arguing.

Phil 2:14

Do not return insult for insult. Romans 12:17

The wise and sensible person ignores an insult.
Proverbs 12:16

Speak to each other in peace (harmony), with celebration, and delicate gracefulness, making melody in your hearts. Ephesians 5:19

Shod your feet with the gospel of peace. (Ephesians 6:15)

As we go to each other in peace, we avoid fights with each other and can stand firm in whatever may come against us.

We all have sinned or have made mistakes. We are all loved by God and forgiven through Christ Jesus.

When we look for the good in each other it helps us to get along better and feel more peace.

When the eye is good, the whole body is good.
Matthew 6:23

If we look for the bad and have absolute thinking, our speech maybe like this:

> *You always...*

> *You never...*

> *Everyone is...*

> *I always...*

> *I never...*

And they can become a source of argument

(since statements like these, are rarely true).

If we look for the good in each other and use words/speech like:

> *You sometimes...*

> *You often...*

> *You rarely...*

> *Many people...*

> *I often...*

> *I sometimes....*

Statements like these are usually more accurate and truthful.

They can be easier to respond appropriately to and will help with honest and peaceful communication.

They can help us to hear what each other is saying, help us to adjust our speech, and to get along more peacefully.

As we adjust our thinking and speech, the landscape around us changes.

Accepting Responsibility for our thinking and speech will change our lives in the direction we desire.

Speak the truth to one another in love. Ephesians 4:15

Confess your sins to one another and pray for one another, so you may be healed. James 5:16

What to do when you have a disagreement or disagree with someone:

1. *Agree with what you can agree on.*

2. *You might agree to disagree. Or agree to give it some time before discussing again.*

Try thinking: I look for something I can agree with/or help with.

1. *I acknowledge the other person's feelings and needs and tell them what I heard them say or what I understand them to need.*

2. *I do and say what I'm willing to do and I ask God to do the rest.*

3. *If I am unable or I am unwilling to help, I say so. It's ok to say, "No," when I need to.*

How to forgive someone else?

Remember, all have made mistakes.

Choices:

1. Pray for the person. Ask God to convict them of their sin and bless them.

2. Go to the person and tell them what they did to hurt you.

3. If it is something severe or that has happened often, ask them to do something for you to make up for it – to help you forgive them and to help them remember and do differently in the future.

We are children of the most, high God, and are favored and loved. Psalm 82:6

Affirmations for healthy relationships

We think the best of each other. We listen to understand.

We value each other's unique abilities and viewpoints.

We cooperate when we can.

Our "Yes" means yes, and our "No" means No.

We accept our own and each other's limitations.

We do what we can and trust God for the rest.

We ask God for what we want and receive it. Our joy is complete.

Let the peace of God rule in your hearts, to which you were called in one body, and become thankful.
Colossians 3:1

Afterword

It is the imbalance of power that has contributed to problems among us, besides our ignorance of God's word.

Within the marriage relationship of one man and one woman, if something is important to the woman, it's important for the man to listen to the woman, consider it and make some sort of provision for her concern. If something is important to the man, it is important for her to pay attention to his concern and cooperate and help him the best she can. Likewise, if something is important to the child, it is important for parents to listen and learn and make sure the child's needs/concerns are met.

It is important to learn from children because they are innocent, connected to God, and gifts from God.

Scripture says you must believe like a child does, to enter the kingdom of Heaven. Jesus came to us as a baby. Listen to your children for they are the children of the living God!

And if it's important to God, we need to do what God says. All are important! All have *different functions, abilities, and positions.*

A house divided cannot stand! It is in unity that we stand! A unified/listening house (family) listens to each other and has lasting peace. The love is true and not counterfeit. If one person's needs are deemed as more important than the others, regular, destruction is sure to come. Peace comes at a cost and is short-lived in these situations.

God the Father   God the Holy Spirit

Child   God the Word – Jesus Christ

Man   Woman

God the Son (Word) – Jesus

God the Father

God the Holy Spirit

Man

Woman

Child

This is the diamond jewel. As we reflect what our role models of God the Father, God the Holy Spirit and Jesus the child, and when all our needs/concerns as a family are provided for and met, lasting peace and love are present.

It is not counterfeit!

This is humans interacting with God, communicating/working together.

As we work together on earth with God at the same time - seeing the good in and listening to understand each other - addressing all concerns. This is when we have true lasting peace!

Getting kicked out of the garden of Eden signifies not only the fall of humankind, but it also refers to the birth of a child – leaving the womb or leaving heaven to come to earth.

Adam initially wanted to keep the peace with the woman, at the cost of disobeying God. Then he blamed her for sinning. This is where sin comes in - First, with disobedience then with blame.

We cannot serve 2 masters – otherwise, we will love the one and hate the other. Matthew 6:24

This is when we have dissensions and counterfeit peace.

When we obey God's word while seeking to please and get along with each other – This is when, _and only when,_ _we have lasting peace_!

If pleasing others requires us to displease or disobey God, it is something we should NOT do! Otherwise, we will self-destruct!

Only when we obey God, as we seek to please others (as well as ourselves), this is when we have lasting peace!

If we ignore ourselves in the process, we self-destruct too! We become out of balance and get counterfeit peace lasting for only a short period. **When we equally listen, consider, provide for, and address all concerns of God and each other, - This is when we have lasting peace! Leaving God, the other person, or ourselves out of the equation – causes ultimate destruction.**

Additionally, If a Dad or Husband is harsh/offensive with a woman's child, the woman feels the same as if he was that way with her, herself. She will tend to be offended and resent it until the man repairs the relationship with the child – And perhaps vice versa. The man may resent the woman in the same scenario until the woman makes things right with the man's child.

The fighting will probably continue until the relationship with the child/ren is repaired. Men acknowledge the hurt to both her and her child! It would be helpful for the woman to acknowledge any of her or her child's disobedience to the man's word and the hurt that is done to him, as well. This is when more lasting peace will come!

The people who are favored by God, seek God and obey/follow His word and are led by the Holy Spirit of God. We all have a choice to do so.

As we work together to repair relationships and follow as God's word says in a spirit of love by listening for understanding, it is then that we have lasting peace!

The world issues begin at home. How many times has a mother sided with a son or a father sided with a daughter because of the harshness of the other parent? This has led to betrayal and suffering. This has caused

It is when the mother and father take responsibility for their actions and work together as a team in line with God's word for all involved, that unity and reoccurring peace are created.

We are the creators of unity ad peace in our world as we follow God's word and own responsibility for our actions, attitudes, and see and believe ourselves, others, and God to be "good."

Covering up secrets also breeds contempt, resentment, and dissension!

No secrets should exist between ourselves - husbands/wives.

No secrets should exist between husband/child - against wife.

<u>No</u> secrets should exist between wife/child – against the husband.

<u>This also breeds contempt, resentment, and dissension!</u>

This is like what Adam and Eve did in the garden of Eden. Satan (the snake) was the tempter. Eve and Adam made a secret agreement against what God said. Then Adam tried to blame Eve for his disobedience. And then they both tried to cover it up. This is what caused them to become ashamed and to fall from God's provision and presence - to have to struggle and work hard and to be without.

We can restore/return to a type of garden of Eden on earth by understanding this and by including God's word (written, spoken, and inspired) into our daily lives and our relationships. God will speak with us as we speak with him.

As we listen to each other and address the concerns of all involved, while staying within

the boundaries God has established (while including God and God's concerns), it is then and only then, that we truly WIN! And have long-lasting reoccurring peace!

We have access to communion with God through being made right through Christ and God's gift of his Holy Spirit. When we are known by God, obey and listen to God, we have communion with God.

It is then that we can ask questions and ask for direction and God hears us and answers us. We live with God and God lives with/among us.

There is nothing we can't have that is good. We are good because God lives in us if we have accepted God's son as our savior and asked God to live in us. God is good!

God doesn't want us to eat from the tree of good _and_ evil (Evil in our hearts, thoughts, or tongue - appearing good.) because it brings destruction, death, and separation from God.

We are only to eat from and practice the good!

This is when we have life abundantly - where all our needs are met, and we share our lives in truth, love, and peace with each other -

trusting in the "Faithful One" to supply all we need and truly desire! This is when we have it all! Serve God, love each other and everything else falls into place.

As we:

1. Look/search for the good in God and each other and ourselves.
2. Honor our own and God's will/word and the will/word of others.
3. Speak the truth in love with each other.
4. Love each other, no more or less than ourselves.
5. Honor ourselves as God's creation, we are all valuable and unique.
6. Follow what God's word says.
7. Accept/know Jesus Christ as our rectifier with God and the one who was first obedient & God's words were in him. He showed us the way and made it possible for the garden of Eden and a right relationship with God to be restored to all of us who might believe in and accept

him as Lord and Savior of our
lives.

8. Listen to understand. Listen to
the Holy Spirit and each other.
Read God's word daily. Do
your best to cooperate and
follow when you can.
Communicate concerns with
each other and God. Listen and
receive.

9. Use your tongue not to destroy
and kill each other, but to heal,
restore, and give life to each
other! Share what you have!

This is when we have reoccurring peace and
communion with God and everything we need
is provided in our daily lives on earth, as it
will be in heaven.

Affirmations for peace:

We have peace, purpose, and plenty.

I know what to do and do it.

*I know God's word/will and
follow it.*

I trust and have faith.

*Abundance and well-being flow into
my/our existence.*

My inner peace radiates joy and confidence.